What Aces Up Your Sleeve?

2016

The Basic Essentials
for Bringing Your Initiatives to Fruition

From the same author:

Quels biscuits avez-vous en poche ? Faites réussir vos initiatives, utilisez le juste nécessaire !, 2016, www.lulu.com

Project Management Momento, Stages and Gates, 2014, www.lulu.com

Manuel à l'usage des chefs de projet qui ont des parties prenantes difficiles, 2005-2015, www.lulu.com

What Aces Up Your Sleeve?

2016

The Basic Essentials
for Bringing Your Initiatives to Fruition

Pascal LE DELEY, PMP®

This booklet can be used as a workbook. You can note down:

Your name:

Starting date:

Expected due date:

Name of your initiative:

Published by:
Pascal LE DELEY, PMP®,
55 rue Etienne Dolet, F-94600 CHOISY LE ROI,
E-mail: retourexperience@aol.com

First impression: May 2014.

PMP® (Project Management Professional) is a registered trademark of Project Management Institute, Inc.
ADKAR® and the terms "Awareness Desire Knowledge Ability Reinforcement" are registered trademarks of Prosci, Inc. The Model ADKAR® is used with permission from Prosci, Inc.
OPPM™ is a registered trademark by Clark Campbell.

The author welcomes corrections and comments on his book. Please feel encouraged to send comments on typographical, formatting, or other errors or improvements. Simply note in an E-mail the relevant page and line of the book, describe the error or improvement and send the E-mail to:
retourexperience@aol.com.

Revision of the 2016 edition: 10 9 8 7 6 5 4 3

ISBN 978-1-326-42565-4

We go from beginning to beginning
by beginnings which have no endings.
Gregory of Nyssa, 331-394.

I dedicate this book to
Marie-Cécile,
Matthieu, Timothée and Sophie.

Foreword

What is an initiative if not a proposition to undertake something? Within a commercial business or a non-profit organization, whether public or private venture, people perceive latent needs. When they feel motivated to act on these needs, their reflection on these initiatives is of the sort: "We want to achieve such and such a result." The germination of these initiatives is, however, not always obvious.

Stages in the life of an initiative

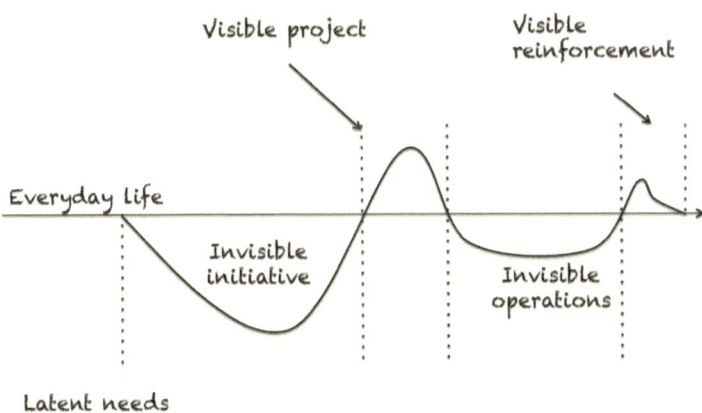

Certain initiatives become visible projects: when an initiative matures, the initiators think of it this way: "We want to obtain this result by launching that project." The big boss may or may no accept launching and sponsoring the project.

In the course of the project, the players of the initiative bring in changes to the operations. At the end of the project, new operations begin their life on a daily basis, in a way that was not necessarily obvious at the start.

After some time, and when the operations become more of a business-as-usual, the sponsors of the original initiative can be reassured that the objectives of the initiative have been reached. This is the stage of the visible reinforcement of the initiative.

This is how the initiative, which is not obvious at the outset, becomes a reality; what the project has achieved and its subsequent reinforcement lead to the noticeable and visible fruition of the initiative.

Contents

Introduction

We have all that is required in the here and now to lead a more fruitful life, to improve our working methods, to deliver better products to our customers. We have what it takes to live happily in the present moment knowing we are more than well-equipped to prepare a better world for our children. I believe we can succeed in our initiatives by applying the basic essentials and thus economizing time and energy which can be dedicated to other aspects of our life. That is how I have been working with project stakeholders since I was a junior project manager.

Why should you read this book?

Because initiatives are born every day. Because all initiatives do not endure. Because an initiative changes something in the environment in which we live. Because certain changes are vital, and for all that, may fail. Because you are not the only one concerned; you must collaborate with others. Because you, on your own, can feel responsible without anyone telling you what to do.

What can you find for yourself in this book?

How to understand your environment and your place in this environment. How to identify with others which initiatives to launch effectively. How to bring success to your chosen initiative and make the success last over time. How to provide your community with sufficient agility in order to be able to adapt to a mobile and changing world. How to save time and energy and be more available for what has meaning for yourself.

I work from the principle that we implement an initiative in order to change something in our environment. The theme of this workbook concerns the management of change produced by an initiative, its impact on people, its repercussions on their responsibilities and on their activities. My inspiration in these pages comes from ADKAR®, a change management model described by Jeffrey M. Hiatt from the company Prosci, which describes the different stages of change and how to negotiate them.

Why choose the "workbook" method? This note-taking system is not merely about conceptual understanding, but because it entails meeting the stakeholders in the field, it facilitates real confrontation. Certain books may be sufficient in themselves, but things are different in project management, where everything can be understood at a glance in a conceptual way, but inefficient if not put into practice in the real context. I have adopted a formula in three stages: a short presentation; a guided experience in the field; and feedback. Here in this workbook, you can accomplish the first two stages. If you follow the stages and procedures in the workbook, you will avoid many a pitfall, you will communicate more easily with the stakeholders, and thus, you will facilitate the success of your initiatives.

When you tackle an initiative you will meet difficulties. This workbook has been designed to smooth them out. However, is there any particular difficulty that stands out above the others? Most certainly the one where you have to collaborate with another person, be interested in them, interview them and understand them. I hope this workbook will give you guidance in how to achieve this, and help you share your experiences in order to gain experience together.

In these pages, I am sharing with you what I myself have received. My aim is to make available to you, through the blending of my contacts and experience, the basic essentials for succeeding in your initiatives and your projects. I have had access to works by the best authors, whom I've echoed as faithfully as possible. If any errors remain, in view of what I owe them, I alone will be held responsible.

1. Discovery questionnaire

You have your place in the environment.

Hypothesis: you act, you make decisions. You have your own objectives and your objectives exceed those of your position, of your organization; you have a certain autonomy (management of your activities, your time, your resources...); you have good reason to act rationally, even though you are limited by the time, by available information, etc.; you experience uncertainties that you strive to reduce; finally, you have a real power, you lead certain people to do what they would not have done without your asking them. In a nutshell, you are a player.

own objectives

a minimum of autonomy

Players have...   bounded rationality

uncertainties

power

Tool — discover yourself as a player with the following set of questions:

How do you act?

Discovery
questionnaire   Where is the difficulty?

Who do you work with?

Invitation (1/2). Consider your environment today, and answer the three questions on the following pages.

How do you act? Describe a typical day, how you start, etc. Your concrete actions, rather than your job definition.

Where is the difficulty? There is always something difficult in what we do. What is it? What do you find challenging?

Who do you work with? Which people, which groups? Designate below the people and the groups you work with. You may use lists, flow-charts, "potato" shapes, relationship diagrams, etc.

Invitation (2/2). Go and meet your colleagues. Start off informally with the people who are the closest to you and work hands-on on the subject, or on the machine, or in regards to the information you have.

We are working with three types of people: the sponsors, the supervisors and the operational staff. The sponsors are the people with power within the organization who take responsibility for the initiatives and provide the means to succeed. The supervisors are the managers who deal with people and the resources of the organization. The operators are the players who transform the subject or information into something of value.

Meet people individually. In the case of a project, it would be legitimate to have a formal interview. However, at this stage, an informal approach is sufficient.

Let's focus on a typical day of the people you are talking to: what they do, what they find difficult, who they work with. Try and identify each relationship (is it cordial? is it tense?) and note down its intensity (strong or weak).

In practice, the interview lasts between ¾ of an hour and 2 hours. This is an important factor in arranging the interview. Here is how I go about it personally: I suggest a slot of ¾ of an hour at a time when it's possible to run over time; a few minutes before the finishing time, I ask the person how they would like to proceed. Most of the time they wish to go on with the interview. For certain people, this will be the first time that someone listens to them in this kind of situation.

Here we are talking, not about the past (past jobs, past difficulties, past relationships), but about the present moment: we need to feel the contact with present reality in order to better understand what's going on. Moreover, memory is known to be selective about a past situation.

Can these interviews be done on the telephone? At the outset, it is preferable to be present with the person in order to perceive completely what the person is communicating. The face-to-face interview is irreplaceable.

"And will I get the cold shoulder?" This rarely happens. As your experience of interviews goes on, your reputation as a good listener will precede you. Most of the time, the interview will take place and will be a shared pleasure.

2. Overall feedback experience: where do we start?

Your environment tells a story.

Initiative provokes change. Before changing anything, begin by considering your environment. In your environment, there are results and ways of doing things; there are things to be proud of and things to be done in a better way. Note down all of this.

What is the reason for evaluating the work context which gives birth to an initiative? Because if you describe the situation at the start, you will be able to show what difference the initiative has made at the finish, and its ultimate value. The consumer, the user or the buyer, by comparing start with finish, will be able to appreciate more deeply the fruits of the initiative, the solution to the problem and the benefits of the change.

Now for the exercise — On the following pages, describe how things are presently being done in your environment.

Our results which are satisfactory and which should be rendered permanent:

Our results which are unsatisfactory and which we have to improve:

....

....

....

....

....

....

....

....

....

....

....

....

....

....

....

....

....

....

....

Our operating methods which work and need to be reinforced:

Our operating methods which can be improved:

....

....

....

....

....

....

....

....

....

....

....

....

....

....

....

....

....

....

....

Ideally, you should conduct this feedback in a group situation, with people who seem interested in your initiative or future project. We will call "stakeholders" the people who are impacted either positively or negatively by your initiative or its results. Look at the organization charts that you drew up before, pick out the stakeholders and invite them to give you their feedback. Start off with an informal but deft approach.

"He who does, is he who knows." So, if in this initiative, you are not the person who does or knows, you are a deputy of those who do and know. Listen and understand what they say; that's how they'll start legitimizing you as the initiative leader.

Continue with the exercise: These meetings have clarified and enriched your perceptions. Collectively describe the initiative which seems pertinent by referring to appendix 8. If several initiatives come to light, refer to appendix 8 as many times as necessary. Keep in mind that, if all the description headings are not immediatly clear, you can come back to add to them at a later time.

3. Grid of objectives

The sponsors of the initiative have their objectives.

The sponsors are recognised by the following attributes:

1- **Power**: they are characters rather high up in the hierarchy — this may give one the feeling that they are unattainable.

2- **Resources**: they provide resources out of the organization they lead, or by delegation/negotiation, in the form of skilled people's time and effort, things, tools or budgets.

3- **Personal interest**: I am talking about their individual interest in the success of the initiative, rather than an interest a group a people may have. In groups, everyone is responsible but no one takes responsibility should a problem arise.

Each initiative needs at least one sponsor. Who is going to give a formal existence to the project? The sponsor. Who is going to provide the resources for the success of the project? Yet again, the sponsor. Who is going to make the key decisions, if not the sponsor? Here is what we can expect of a sponsor. He or she:

• decides to launch the initiative,

• announces the launching of the project to the stakeholders,

• provides their support for the efforts already committed,

• reinforces the operational changes.

Search the potential sponsors among the stakeholders, that is, those who have the attributes mentioned above. Once you have identified them, these people will indicate to you the objectives they are seeking. Then, together, check how the initiative in question helps meet their objectives. This is a powerful means to confront the sponsors, who are the deciders, with the evidence that we must make this initiative succeed!

For example: in a specific business unit, the success of such an initiative has an influence on *client satisfaction* and a direct impact on the *respect for deadlines*; in addition, this initiative indirectly contributes to *respecting the budget* and directly to the *viability of the service.*

Invitation. Validate the presence or the absence of the three attributes for each stakeholder of the initiative. Then identify the sponsor or the sponsors. If there are several, coordinate the sponsors.

Stakeholders	Powers?	Resources?	Interests?	Sponsors?

Some sponsors are unaware of the fact that the initiative in question concerns them. In this case, you can sell the idea of the initiative to the sponsor by coaching this person, even though they may have a very high position in the hierarchy. They may be very grateful to you. Perhaps 'coach' is too strong a word, but you can, at the very least, indicate to this person what the team in charge of the initiative is expecting of them.

Exercise: Assess the needs of the business unit with the sponsors. Then evaluate the contribution your initiative is going to make in relation to these objectives. Then corroborate with your sponsors on your conclusions.

If your sponsors belong to the same organization, one table will be sufficient. If several business units are concerned, you will have to fill in a table for each one, then sell the initiative to each business unit sponsor separately as being essential to their success.

Objectives	1	2	3	4	5

Legend:
1 = The initiative is optional in order to reach the objective.
2 = The initiative contributes indirectly to reaching the objective.
3 = The initiative contributes directly to achieving the objective.
4 = The initiative is fundamental to reaching the objective.
5 = The objective cannot possibly be reached if the initiative fails.

When you meet the sponsor, you will know what will become of your initiative: if the sponsor is half-hearted, so will be the initiative; if the sponsor is energetic, the initiative will be energetic also. When you cannot get around a situation on your own and you call on the support of a sponsor (the principle of 'escalation') you'll find out where you are: an energetic sponsor will come to a clear decision (in accordance with the information you have given him) and your initiative rapidly stands more of a chance to succeed; on the contrary...

Like any player, sponsors have limited, bounded rationality, depending on the information they have (too much or too little), on how much time they can devote to the study, on the constraints which hold them back, on their cognitive capacity of reacting to the knowledge of the moment, their intellectual leanings, their beliefs, their health and on their mood. You should be sympathetic towards them. I have met many a person who has often been badly informed, aware of not being able to act by themselves, under the pressure of making a providential decision, and finally being uncertain of how their directive is about to be taken into account.

What to do if the sponsors have already given their approval and the project has already been given the go-ahead weeks or months ago? It may happen that the context of the initiative has evolved and no longer has the pertinence it had in the beginning. It may be that the initiative has been launched without assembling the people, the different energies and the information necessary for a good beginning. When you are in charge of a project which has already been formalized, hold meetings to discover who the stakeholders are that you are meeting for the first time (ch. 1), make an appraisal of their feedback (ch. 2) and validate the information about the stakeholders (ch. 3-4) and about initiative alignment with the objectives (ch. 3). If this information is not available, go and gather it up, as if you were starting off the initiative. In other words, meet up with the stakeholders, validate the available information and fill in any information you may need.

4. Stakeholders' register

The stakeholders consider the change.

Take an interest in the stakeholders in order to discover progressively how these people perceive what is at stake. Do it before you really need to, so that, when you require help or the specific participation of one of stakeholders, you are already in contact with them; this always makes things easier.

Draft a first analysis of the stakeholders and spend some time discussing and sharing it with the sponsor. For each stakeholder, share information on:

1-The identity of the stakeholder

2-Their interest, what their biggest concerns are and what they are remunerated for

3-The impact that the initiative could have on them

4-The impact the stakeholder could have on the initiative

5-How you imagine going about diminishing the risk of failure or increasing the chances of success in relation to this stakeholder

6-How you are going to communicate with this stakeholder

Stakeholder register

STAKEHOLDERS	Stakeholders' INTERESTS	Stakeholders' IMPACTS on the initiative

Stakeholder register (cont.)

IMPACTS the initiative has on stakeholders	STRATEGIES to adopt in relation to the stakeholders	Means of COMMUNICATION with stakeholders

As you can see, these people are good at their job and do it well. They are able to transform subject matter or unprocessed information into something of value. They deserve our respect. No matter what, things are under control; certainly well enough to assure the basics, but perhaps not enough to be totally satisfied, hence the initiative.

It may well be that each person misconstrues what other players in their environment experience. Your role is to help them rediscover their interdependence in relation to the other players. Your mission is one of coordination.

So that the initiative succeeds, the operators must effect the change induced by the initiative: otherwise it remains idealistic and sterile. Some fear such a change, others look forward to it. This results in the following uncertainties: Are the operators going to collaborate? Is the initiative going to be successful? Or rather, what do we have to do to make it succeed? We will now take a look at these questions.

5. Motivation questionnaire for stakeholders

Is the initiative viable?

Taking initiative implies making choices which in turn could lead to making sacrifices. So you have to convince the stakeholders that the initiative they are preparing to undertake with you is more viable and more attractive than anything else they are busy with.

Before convincing them, make some investigations.

Here are four key questions that any stakeholder may ask before saying "yes, I'll participate":

1- Do I have an imperative need to react? Imperative in the sense of fearing the worst if the initiative fails.

2- Do I have the means, the skills, the resources and the capabilities to succeed? All these things, even though they are lacking, could be (easily) solved by a sponsor, a trainer, a coach or a mentor.

3- Can this new project be more important than my other duties, my other obligations and my other projects?

4- Finally, does my participation compare with the problems I may incur? What's in it for me?

Four times "yes" means that the stakeholder is ready to participate. A single "no" means there is hesitation and they need to be convinced.

Invitation. Complete the analysis of the stakeholders and discuss it with the sponsor until you reach some kind of agreement. For each stakeholder:

0- Is the stakeholder a sponsor?

1- To what degree do they have imperative needs for participating?

2- What are their capabilities?

3- How will the initiative eventually affect other activities?

4- Is the challenge worthwhile for them?

Stakeholder register (cont.)

STAKEHOLDERS	Is the stakeholder a SPONSOR?	IMPERATIVE reasons for participating?

Stakeholder register (end)

What are their CAPABILITIES?	How will this affect their OTHER ACTIVITIES?	Is it WORTHWHILE for them?

Introduction to the ADKAR® Model

Supported by numerous observations and research, Jeffrey HIATT has created the ADKAR® Model in order to facilitate change in any organization. The efficacy of this model is mainly based, in my opinion, on the identification of the stakeholders as three hierarchical types: the sponsor, the supervisor, and the operator. It indicates how to deal with these participants in the occurrence of a change.

There are 5 stages in the ADKAR® Model:

1- Awareness

2- Desire

3- Knowledge

4- Ability

5- Reinforcement

Concepts in Prosci's *ADKAR: A Model For Change In Business, Government and Our Community.*

The following chapters are dedicated to the practical use of this model.

6. Discourse on awareness (A for Awareness)

The sponsor communicates his awareness of the change.

Communication from the sponsor is, of course, communication from the top down.

With the 'elevator pitch' (appendix) you have convinced the sponsor to play his/her part which is to get the initiative underway and make this known to the stakeholders. Jeffrey M. HYATT in the ADKAR® Model indicates that someone in a situation of change expects the person at the top (a sponsor) to show him/her the objectives to reach in four points:

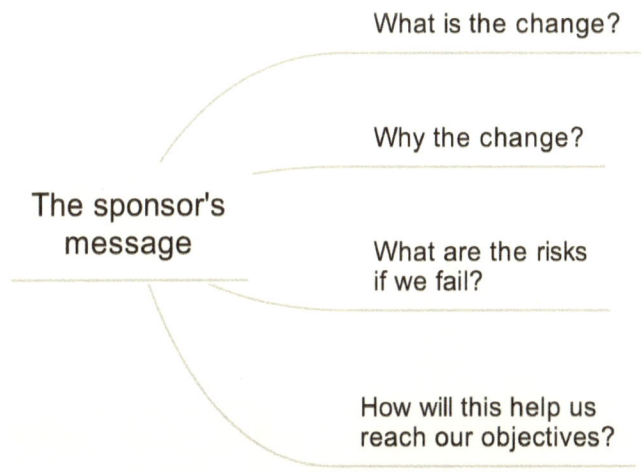

What is the change?

Why the change?

The sponsor's message

What are the risks if we fail?

How will this help us reach our objectives?

Image based on concepts in Prosci's
ADKAR: A Model For Change In Business, Government and Our Community.

In this first step of the ADKAR® Model, *'Awareness'*, it is up to the sponsor to communicate the necessity for change.

Invitation. Write a first message « Awareness of the change » and discuss with the sponsor until you are in complete agreement.

What is the change? What does the change, the initiative or the project involve?

Why are we embarking on this change?

What risks are we taking if we fail to make the change?

How will the success of this change help us reach our objectives?

NB. Here you have the test to validate the choice of sponsors for the initiative. If these sponsors are happy to embark on the initiative, and if the prospect of the project incites them to proclaim out loud the substance of these 4 points, you have effectively found your sponsors. If it's not the case, keep on looking!

Don't go on unless the sponsor has formally communicated his/her Awareness message. The success of further stages depends on the completion of Awareness.

7. Analysing the changes (D for Desire)

Supervisors construct the desire for change.

Initiative implies work and responsibility changes, possible troubles and possible gains.

Some of the stakeholders are just waiting for the change to happen and others not, the latter expressing the widely held idea of "resistance to change". We must mistrust our propensity to filter the facts which go against our convictions; if I am convinced of a" resistance to change" I could underestimate the stakeholders who desire change. There are certainly people who are not only ready for change but also who ardently desire it.

For certain stakeholders, the initiative increases their uncertainties; they wonder how they can cope with this even greater uncertainty without losing face. For others, the initiative totally solves the problem they had to deal with and hence they worry about justifying their function. Finally, the initiative can reduce uncertainties pertinent to some stakeholders' work; they are ready to accept it.

The developers of the ADKAR® Model highlight the fact that the desire for change can be built up and that the architects of this desire are the direct supervisors of the operators concerned. These operators are intrigued to find out what the initiative changes for them, accompanied by a supervisor who understands and supports them:

1-What's in it for all of us?

2-What's in it for me?

3-How does it change my work activities?

4-How does it change my responsibilities?

Based on concepts in Prosci's *ADKAR: A Model For Change In Business, Government and Our Community*.

Invitation. Draw up a first version of the impact and the benefits for each stakeholder.

What's in it for all of us?

What's in it for me?

How does it change my work activities?

How does it change my responsibilities?

Example: using this workbook can result in developing more frequent and close relationships, which fosters mutual understanding and fruitful collaboration. Personally speaking, I feel surer of myself in gaining the trust of the operators as they feel I am fully taking them into consideration. I once made a decision: each morning I'd greet each one, I'd arrange appointments (no more than three a day) with the people I have not yet met. This way, I feel that each person I listen to knows that I am taking into account what they tell me about the initiative or anything else that matters; on the other hand, I am responsible for clarifying what has to be dealt with in the context of the initiative and what one has to expect from a new opportunity.

Strengthened by these discovery interviews,

1- try and analyse what the impact (on activities and responsibilities) could be, and the benefits (for the team or the individual), for each stakeholder of the initiative, and

2- interview each one for confirmation in collaboration with their supervisor. This could possibly be a second round.

Where to begin? Start by the operators closest to the ground and work bottom-up, the same approach as in the discovery of the environment (ch. 1-2).

Why talk about desire? Because people may think they want change but at the deepest level are reticent to really desire it. Consciously, they are persuaded that change is a good thing whereas their sometimes unconscious desire may hold them back. It is quite frequent that we are unable to realize a goal that we want but which we don't deeply desire (I want to move to bigger a city for better job opportunities, however I'd prefer to live in my village among my friends). And the other way around as well, it's not uncommon that we don't want something while unconsciously desiring it (even though I don't want to be at risk riding a motorbike, I'd like to own one).

8. Training for change (K for Knowledge)

At this stage, the operators are aware that something is changing and desire to participate in the change. There are new tasks they have to perform in their changing job. Now is the time for the training necessary to the success of the initiative, "Knowledge" in the ADKAR® model. Without the appropriate knowledge, even the most motivated of the operators might fail in their new functions.

Training involves:

- Senior operators, who prepare and lead the training session, or encourage the trainees

- Junior operators who dedicate some time to training, who listen, take notes or implement by themselves

There are three ways to train the operators in the tasks that they must perform in their new job: we can evoke, explain or implement. *Discussions* take a few minutes, *explanations* about 10 minutes and *implementations* more or less an hour.

At the outset of the training design, as you are building up the training session timetable (what to do first, what to do next, etc.), how can you figure out which are the tasks to be evoked, explained or implemented? By calculating the following index for each one.

Index = Importance + Difficulty – (2 x Experience)

Refer to the following table for the values to be used.

Score	I **Importance for business**	D **Learning Difficulty**	E **On-the-job Experience**
Low (0 point)	It's good to have; it makes a difference, but it will go unnoticed.	If it is explained over the phone, I'll manage.	I have the required information; I've done it once without any telling result, or I've never done it.
Medium (1 point)	It makes a difference; managers have noticed.	I need training or coaching in order to succeed.	I've done it more than once; the result was acceptable.
High (2 points)	It makes a difference; the clients have noticed.	I need training AND coaching in order to succeed.	My colleagues say I have the know-how, and trust me to succeed.
Very high (3 points)	We can't do business without it.	I need a hands-on learning experience (like learning to fly a plane) in order to succeed.	I'm successful in training people how to succeed in carrying out the task.

Task index = 4 or above? The learners must *implement* this task, as they lack the experience to negotiate the change of task by themselves.

Task index = 1, 2 or 3? *Give explanations*.

Task index = 0 or below? It is sufficient *to simply discuss* the issue as the learners have sufficient experience to deal with the task.

Example. Say a task is 'translate an owner's manual from English to German'. People tell you that they have those customers in Germany (importance is very high), that on-line translators simply don't do the job (difficulty is high), and that most people in their group have not practiced translation since high school (experience is low). So, Importance=3, Difficulty=2, Experience=0,

$$\text{Task index} = 3 + 2 - (2 \times 0) = 5$$

Since 'translate an owner's manual from English to German' task index is above 4, you should plan for *implementing* this task during the session.

From this you will get training activities ranging from *implementations* (each one lasting more or less an hour), *explanations* (about 10 minutes) to simple *discussions* (a few minutes). As you are building up the training session timetable, put *implementation* building blocks up front and then introduce *explanations* and fill the remaining time with the *discussions*. You will be able to work out how much time you need for a training session (hours? days?).

Invitation. Ask the senior operators how they deal with the new tasks involved and about their desire and ability to transfer knowledge. With those willing to teach, make out a list of tasks necessary for the new situation at hand and calculate the score of each one by referring to the table.

"Job experience" refers to the trainees' experience, assuming that trainees form a homogeneous group. If the trainees form a rather heterogeneous group, split them in two homogeneous groups, or more.

Arrange to conduct the training in the ten days prior to introducing the change; otherwise, the new learning may not be retained when it comes time to implement it.

During the training sessions, try to take into consideration the different learning and cognitive capacities of the trainees, whether they be visual (diagrams, helicopter views), auditive (procedures, details) or kinesthetic (hands-on activities, workshop visits).

Translate from English to German   3 2 0 **5**

Task   I   D   E   =

Task   I   D   E   =

Task   I   D   E   =

Task   I   D   E   =

Task   I   D   E   =

Task   I   D   E   =

Task   I   D   E   =

Task   I   D   E   =

Task   I   D   E   =

Task   I   D   E   =

Task   I   D   E   =

Task   I   D   E   =

Task   I   D   E   =

Task   I   D   E   =

Task   I   D   E   =

Task   I   D   E   =

Task . . . . I D E =

Task . . . . I D E =

Task . . . . I D E =

Task . . . . I D E =

Task . . . . I D E =

Task . . . . I D E =

Task . . . . I D E =

Task . . . . I D E =

Task . . . . I D E =

Task . . . . I D E =

Task . . . . I D E =

Task . . . . I D E =

Task . . . . I D E =

Task . . . . I D E =

Task . . . . I D E =

Task . . . . I D E =

Task . . . . I D E =

9. Accompanying the operators (A for Ability)

Operators and supervisors put their *ability* into practice.

A new initiative allows the stakeholders to deal with what comes up by looking to the future. It involves research — you have to be reactive; problems can arise because of the initiative — you have to be tolerant; initiative brings up new situations — you have to be on the lookout; finally, initiative can also generate good surprises — you must show enthusiasm.

As soon as the operators are trained and are back at their workstations, the coaching period begins where you can give them answers to their questions, encourage them to put into practice what they have learned, and correct possible mistakes.

According to the ADKAR® Model, during this stage, the supervisors take on the role of *coach* for the operators; this is a key period in applying the change. You have to help them. In the strict sense of their role, the *coaches* are not there to advise, but to assist the *trainees* in their research so that they come up with their own solution.

> *In a situation of change, the operators are sometimes a bit lost and no longer know how to operate. They look for solutions and try to adapt to a changing situation. In these conditions, you will often be tempted to react in one of two ways: either refraining from going forward unless all the consequences of the change have been foreseen, or focusing on what is already under control and laboriously consolidating as you go along. Be confident; learn as you go.*

Here is a practical model, widely used in coaching.

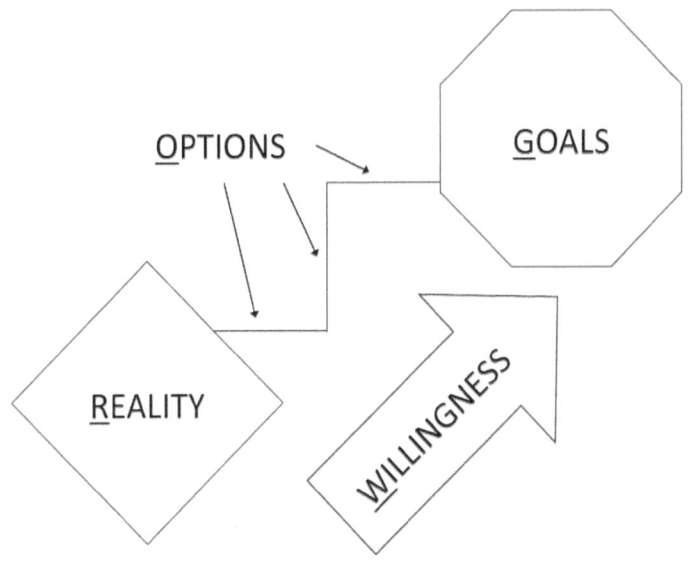

Coaching model adapted from G.R.O.W.

What are the goals? What is the desired result? Let's project ourselves ahead six months or a year and describe what we would like to have achieved by then, G (*Goals*).

From these projections, let's go back to our present situation and describe it, R (*Reality*).

Then, let's ask the question: what have we done to fast-forward from the reality towards the goal. This is about *Options*, looking at several more or less independent stages on the way. In the above diagram, you can see that the options start off from the reality (bottom left-hand corner) climbing up the steps towards the goals (top right-hand corner). Each horizontal or vertical segment represents an initiative.

Finally, let us take into account the willingness and motivation which have been implemented in the different options taken, W (*Willingness*).

10. Reinforcement of the initiative (R for Reinforcement)

The sponsor reinforces the change.

The change has now taken place and the operators are playing the game. After a few months, take the following two steps:

1-Together with the stakeholders, analyse the operational achievement of the initiative.

2-Ask sponsors to intervene and reinforce their approval of the initiative.

Reinforcement corresponds to the word "*Act*" in the *Plan-Do-Check-Act* formula which quality managers are familiar with.

You have succeeded in introducing the change; now take the time to standardize it, rather than treating it as some passing event.

Invitation.

1-Take stock of your collective action by meeting up with the stakeholders, as you have done during the entire process of the initiative.

2-Invite the sponsors to review the achievements of the initiative with the stakeholders during a congratulatory meeting where the success of the stakeholders is to be celebrated.

The following feedback is to be done with the stakeholders, referring to the table "ways of doing things" from Chapter 2 and compared with what you described at the outset of the initiative. This will make the progress which you have achieved much more evident.

When the sponsors have seen the results which have been obtained, they may want to move up a gear. But at the same time, things have evolved, the context, people etc. If and when, on replying to this invitation, you commit yourself to another initiative, start from the very beginning: interviews, discovery, etc.

What are our satisfying results and what must be rendered permanent?

Which results are we not happy with and which can be bettered?

Successful operating methods which we must reinforce.

Our operating methods which can be improved:

Appendices

A. 1 – How to sell an initiative. The elevator pitch

You have discovered an opportunity. You'd like to push an initiative. How can you go about promoting your idea? Let's start off by preparing a speech in order to persuade the people concerned that the initiative is really worth being launched. This is called the "elevator pitch" and here is the plan, according to Isabelle Genest, http://isabellegenest.com/2010/04/15/elevator-pitch-recette-23/.

1-The problem, as in telling a story

2-How the problem has been solved up till now

3-The solution I suggest

4-The benefits for "you" / the client

5-How my proposition differs from the others

6-The action I invite "you" to take

The last point ("the action I invite you to take") is the moment you solicit the opinion of your discussion partner or you ask for an appointment so that you can talk things over more comfortably. The time will come to ask them to be the sponsor of the initiative, where this is appropriate.

Invitation. Prepare your speech using the grid on the following pages.

1 – « The problem », like telling a story.

2 - « How the problem has been solved up till now ».

3 - « The solution I suggest ».

4 - « The benefit for "you" / the client ».

5 - « How my proposition differs from the others ».

6 - « The action I invite "you" to take ».

Elevator pitch example.

"As you know, we use reference substances to control our products before delivery to the client. Do you know that at this very moment, it so happens that certain stocks of reference substances are empty? This has a big impact on the delivery deadlines of our product and, as a result, on customer satisfaction. What's more, we are penalized with a 10% penalty for every lot which suffers a late delivery which means a 10,000 to 50,000€ fine, without taking into consideration the loss of an early-delivery bonus.

"Today, we carry out an analysis 1 to 2 weeks upstream of the delivery date. If we are lacking in reference substances, we have the time to reorder the substances before the delivery date; but out of 20% of all deliveries, the order for reference substances is made *after* the desired delivery date of the product.

"In order to solve this problem, I suggest that we integrate the management of the substance references with that of the products in store, by using the same tool which is used for managing the stock.

"By proceeding in this way, we should avoid the 10,000 to 50,000€ losses because of the reduction of delays in the controls and, as a result, in the delivery, in 99% of the cases. This solution will cost about 8000€ for the software license and the training of the users.

"I will coach individually the operators who are involved and their supervisors before and after their training session to make sure they are completely operational.

"How about finding an ideal time in your schedule so that you can examine this solution and decide whether you would like to entrust us with this improvement project?"

A. 2 – Dealing with a conflict. Five options

The following are the 5 options when dealing with a conflict:

- The forceful 'charge'. "Get out of the building immediately!" Fireman use their authority to take over, and seeing the flames, I'm more than thankful. The "forcing" approach suggests an evaluation of the decision after the fact. If there had been no flames, what indeed would that change? Bitterness instead of gratefulness.

- Easing the tension. Two children are fighting over an apple from their apple tree. They end up by going their own ways without chosing the apple. But why... is the fruit rotten or is it too green? It's not worth fighting over so little, but let us save our energy in order to take up the struggle again when the time is ripe.

- Confrontation. Look for a consensus or a means to negotiate. Take the time, if the situation is really worth the effort.

- Compromise. Take a little, leave a little and so the story goes, for we both wish to move forward. However, what if I realize tomorrow that I'm no longer attached to what I may have gained; and that what I had before was so much more worthwhile to me? Frustration.

- Retreat. I'll yield ground without any further consideration this time. I'll keep my forces for the future. Or else, I quite simply realize my error, "I made a mistake".

Remarks.

Practice the five different approaches, even if you have to train yourself for those that you control the least. Each approach entails some preparation, each approach has its own pertinence but there is no winning formula. Each to their own choice... which one do *you* prefer?

Force and confrontation are certainly both ways of managing a conflict situation, somewhat like firemen who force everyone to leave the burning building. Because of their job and their instinct, they deal with the conflict in a forceful manner, where they are trained to control their emotions. But we are not all capable of managing our emotions in this way, even though with training and experience, we may be able to succeed. Some people have the right kind of psychology to be more active in a conflict, whereas others are more timid and have a tendency to compromise, or even avoid conflict and retreat.

Conflict has of course been a normal component of any organised action since the beginning of *Homo sapiens*, but it doesn't necessarily imply violence. I may be wrong, but I think that it is the absence of the spoken word which induces violence, and not the conflict a such.

A. 3 – Bouncing back after a difficult exchange. Reassessing

Experience in general can be made up of all our experiences. How do we gain from this? By reassessing them. This approach was popularized by Ignatius Loyola (1491-1556) Here are the three stages:

1- What I have done

2- How this has affected me

3- Where I must go from here

You have been involved in an exchange that has affected you; you are preoccupied by this altercation. During the following 24 hours calmly review this interaction for yourself.

By reviewing the situation, you avoid allowing your feelings to make the decisions for you, or allowing them to bother the people around you. But also, by reviewing the situation, you permit your feelings to nurture your decisions.

In going over the situation, we distinguish the way we have acted "what I have done" from our feelings "how this has affected me", and from our decisions "where I must go from here" Our *acts* are in the past, and exist as such. We try to let our *feelings* exist in neutral territory; they precede our will. Our *decisions* depend on our will.

> *Reassess the situation by confiding in someone you trust. There is no lack of opportunity. You will be surprised by how much better you feel and how much more eager you will be to play your role with a greater degree of subtlety. This is especially true if you are in a position of responsibility and without hierarchical authority.*

A. 4 – Communicating in a non-violent manner

Non-violent communication dispels the accusatory approach, liberates dialogue, appeases the conflict and defuses the situation.

1- What has happened? (the facts)

2- How has this affected me? (my feelings)

3- What do I need?

4- What am I asking (you) for?

By reviewing a difficult exchange (cf appendix 3), you have decided to renew communication with the person involved. During the 24 hours which follow the altercation, settle down, look at the questions one by one, and clarify your message. Then, go back and talk to the person in question.

In order to do this, some people will choose to discuss the situation with a trustworthy colleague, others will make notes. Writing things down helps clarify, using these simple rules:

- Be specific: rather than the expression "I feel hurt" look to see if you feel anxious, irritated, angry etc.

- Ask yourself what this situation takes you back to, as in when "I feel humiliated" becomes "I feel like a child being reprimanded"

- Be brief and simple in your preparation for the renewal of contact.

  Why does the approach of non-violent communication work so well? Because it involves verbal communication and avoids the pitfalls caused by the absence of dialogue, i.e. unjustified and violent behavior; because communication can be in the first person — I still have the right to use the word "I" —, and not the second person — the accusatory "you" which destroys the relationship; because it invites self-criticism and allows for empathy.

A. 5 – Preparing a negotiation

For someone in a responsible position but without any hierarchical authority, negotiation is a great solution to obtaining any kind of change. To be successful, a negotiation has to be well prepared. Before the negotiation meeting as such, fill out the table below with information about yourself and about your partner in negotiation.

1- Objectives

2- Values

3- Constraints

4- Thresholds

5- Alternative solutions

At the outset of the meeting, if there is missing information, take some time with your negotiation partner to discover other data you need to know, before discussing things further.

In the absence of an alternative solution, the negotiation stops. Check to make sure that you and your partner both have alternative solutions.

You

Objectives

Values

Constraints

Thresholds

Alternative solutions

YOUR PARTNER

Objectives

Values

Constraints

Thresholds

Alternative solutions

A. 6 – Structuring the minutes of a meeting

Here are the classical categories of the minutes of a weekly team meeting.

- Heading: Minutes of meeting of <committee name> for <name of project> on <date> at <place>
- Those present
- Those excused
- Discussions
- Decisions made
- Upcoming absences/unavailabilities
- Next steps/stages
- Appendices

A. 7 – Questioning
the progress of a deliverable

What activities do you lead with a collaborator in charge of initiative or project deliverables?

- Validate the present production
- Measure the expenses up till now
- Evaluate what remains to be done
- Identify any variances with what was planned (where appropriate)
- Identify the reason for variances
- Check the existence of possible tendencies
- Suggest corrective actions

A. 8 – Summarizing the initiative

The « WHAT »

The « WHY »

The « WHAT FOR »

The « WHEN »

The « HOW »

The « WHERE »

The « WHO »

The « HOW MUCH »

The « BUDGET »

A. 9 – Planning and following a project through

All-on-one-page (OPPM) or in one file (Who, What, When)

I suggest you use the Swiss army knife of project management and reporting: the One Page Project Manager, and to avoid reduplicating the information, I'll leave you to consult the specific website:

https://oppmi.com

Concerning the activities to be undertaken, deliverables to be developed, problems to be solved in order to negotiate a successful outcome to your initiative or project, the vital element is the tool WWW (what, who, when). How does it work?

Register information on each activity, deliverable or problem to be solved in the following model:

WHAT	WHO	WHEN	STATUS
Activity / Deliverable / Problem	Who takes responsibility?	Expected end date or delivery date	Ongoing / Closed / Frozen / Abandoned

Experience shows that, in order to be successful in achieving an activity, completing a deliverable or solving a problem, you must have one person (but not a group) to take the responsibility, a clear unambiguous objective and an end date which is not too far off (a few days or a few weeks). If one of these items is missing, the activity, the deliverable or the problem to be solved will probably not be successful.

To give responsibility to someone who is absent from a meeting is futile. You should only give the responsibility to people who are present at a meeting, even though they may delegate to others afterwards.

At each meeting, take a look at the What, Who, When register from the last meeting, have a discussion about each item and do a collective update on its status. Then create a new series of recordings, one on the activities, one on the deliverables and another on the problems to be solved. Continue the same process from one meeting to the next.

Status updates may look like:

- Ongoing ⇨ Closed
- Ongoing ⇨ Frozen ⇨ Ongoing ⇨ Closed
- Ongoing ⇨ Abandonned

The advantage is that the stakeholders know what is up-front; the disadvantage is that the stakeholders may only pay attention to what is in the dossier and not to what isn't, in the same way as one might forget the butter in the supermarket if it isn't on the shopping list.

A. 10 – Reading material to sharpen your tools. Bibliography

From an engineer's point of view

CAMPBELL C. A., *The One-Page Project Manager: communicate and manage any project with a single sheet of paper*, Hoboken, NJ, John Wiley & Sons, 2007, https://oppmi.com/

HIATT, J. M., *ADKAR: A Model For Change In Business, Government and Our Community*, Loveland, Colorado, Prosci Learning Center Publications, 2006

PMI (Coll.), *A guide to the Project Management Book of Knowledge (PMBOK)*, Fifth edition, Project Management Institute, Inc., Newtown Square, Pennsylvania, USA, 2013

From a sociological aspect

ALLISON G., ZELIKOW P., *Essence of Decision, Explaining the Cuban Missile Crisis*, 2° edition, NY, NY, USA, Addison Wesley Longman, Inc., 1999

For an efficient culture in project management

BOLLES R.N., *What Color is your Parachute? A practical manual for job-hunters and carreer-changers*, Berkeley, Ten Speed Press, 1992-2015

DOBELLI R., *The Art Of Thinking Clearly*, Sceptre, Hodder & Stroughton, London, 2013

My own beliefs

Through my experiences and what I have gained from them, I have come to acquire certain beliefs which change my way of seeing and doing things. This workbook is influenced by those beliefs. To be honest and useful, I will describe them to you, as you will have, no doubt, your own, and some of them may be in accordance. Let me give voice to mine.

Hic et nunc, here and now, we are given everything we need for living a happy and fruitful life.

Man is basically good. I assume my referential basis as Judeo-Christian.

People have good reason to act as they do. I do too. They have a particular point of view which is incomplete. So is mine.

Leadership is something to be learned. Listen to your discussion partner with attention and try and understand before expecting to be understood yourself. Giving him/her consideration is the first step towards leadership.

It's far better to have an imperfect product which is available than a perfect product which is not.

Eight times out of ten, misunderstandings are based on our different cognitive preferences. Either draw up a visual plan, give auditive details, or visit the workshop with the tactile and kinesthetic.

The one who does is the person who knows, therefore I empower the ones who do.

The operators are the ones who create the value and who remunerate the others. It is our role to clear the operator's path of obstacles.

It is much better to act with someone than to act for them. The result comes from a shared effort, which is what matters, even though it may not be perfect.

My mission is to make my clients' customers happy. My client will be satisfied when their customers place orders more and more often, thanks to my efforts.

Work is a source of pride, pleasure and joy.

Beyond a certain stage, and in order to advance further down the path, I would feel much happier lightening my bag than weighing it down even more. Simplify down to the basic essentials.

Glossary

ADKAR®. A model for accompanying change within an organization, developed by Jeffrey M. HIATT, *Cf.* Bibliography.

Desire. A strong wish to obtain or to do something.

GROW. Acronym designating a process of coaching in four stages: Goals, Reality, Options and Willingness.

Initiative. A proposition to undertake something.

Operations. A programmed production of regular actions in order to assure the daily workings of an enterprise.

Operator. Someone who operates a process or a machine.

Player. Individual or group of individuals, who decide and act and whose decisions and actions influence the initiative or project.

Project. A temporary enterprise with the view to producing a novelty, product or service.

Sponsor. A person interested in backing and bringing a project to fruition, who has power in the environment and who has the capacity to decide and allocate resources.

Stakeholders. People interested one way or another, positively or negatively in the initiative/project or the results of the aforesaid initiative/project.

Supervisor. Person in charge of managing the operators.

Will. A firm intention to do something.

Acknowledgements

To Pascal Bohn PMP®, PgMP®, for the hours of conversation, shared experiences, and our work in common,

To my collaborators on diverse projects, who asked me to put things in black and white during our lively discussions, our shared experiences, and our most useful discussions on project management,

To the students of Lille (Administrative Institute of Enterprises, Superior Institute of Agriculture and the Superior Institute of Electronics and Numericals), of Angers (Institute of Science and Engineering Techniques of Angers) and of Paris-Est Creteil University, whose questions push me each year to continue with the work in progress,

To my colleagues, project managers with Air Liquide, Areva, Galderma, IBM, Michelin, Renault, Schneider Electric, and so many others, who form a passionate community with much solidarity, and which I feel honored to belong to,

To Jennifer Boyson, Atul Dhanorker and Lacey Hart (Mayo Clinic, Rochester, Minnesota) who welcomed me into their *Project Management Office* and who keep sharing tools, techniques and insights with me,

To Pierre-Guy Duny (Areva) who instilled in me the virus of basic essentials,

To Denis Fenouillet, Dominique Joly et Maurice Testu (SNCF), who shed light for me on the daily life of a big Parisian railway station,

To Yup (T- Systems) and Peter Alty (Eurocontrol), whose contact sealed my optimism for our profession,

To Gilles Leblanc and Régis Moilleron of the Paris-Est Creteil University who supported my approach to basic essentials and project management,

To the professionals who shared their personal experience about quality with me,

To the collaborators of Project Management Global Solutions (PMGS) directed by Stéphane Derouin, who entrusted me to lead training sessions on project management during which I met many a colleague,

To Krisanne Novak and Marc Robert, without whom the contents of this workbook would not be so accessible and precise,

To Chuck McNeal, Jeremy Carson (Prosci) and Jeffrey Larson-Keller (Mayo Clinic, Rochester, Minnesota) who taught me how to use the ADKAR® Model in real life situations,

To Anton Elder, for his faithful friendship and the translation from French,

To Marie-Cécile, the encounter with whom is the best thing that ever happened to me,

My gratitude and joy in transmitting and sharing what I have received from you all.

www.ingramcontent.com/pod-product-compliance
Lightning Source LLC
Chambersburg PA
CBHW021900170526
45157CB00005B/1907